10 Trim-the-Tree'ers

To my grandson, Max
—J.S.

To my sister, Aggles,
with love
—L.D.

10 Trim-the-Tree'ers

a holiday counting book

by Janet Schulman • illustrated by Linda Davick

SCHOLASTIC INC.

10 little neighbors
about to trim their tree.
They'll dress for the occasion.

Turn the page and see!

1 shiny golden star
at the very tip-top.

2 strings of flashing lights
that just won't stop.

3 little angels with halos
and with wings.

4 Santa's elves making toys that he brings.

5 swift reindeer—they know how to fly.

6 lacy snowflakes
that fall from the sky.

7 jolly men all made of snow.

8 candy canes—no eating them, though!

9 menorah candles to mark the gift of light.

10 pretty presents to make our holiday bright.

10 trim-the-tree'ers,
now their job is done.
It's time to serenade
their pets and everyone.

We wish you a merry Christmas,
We wish you a merry Christmas,
We wish you a merry Christmas,
And a happy New Year.

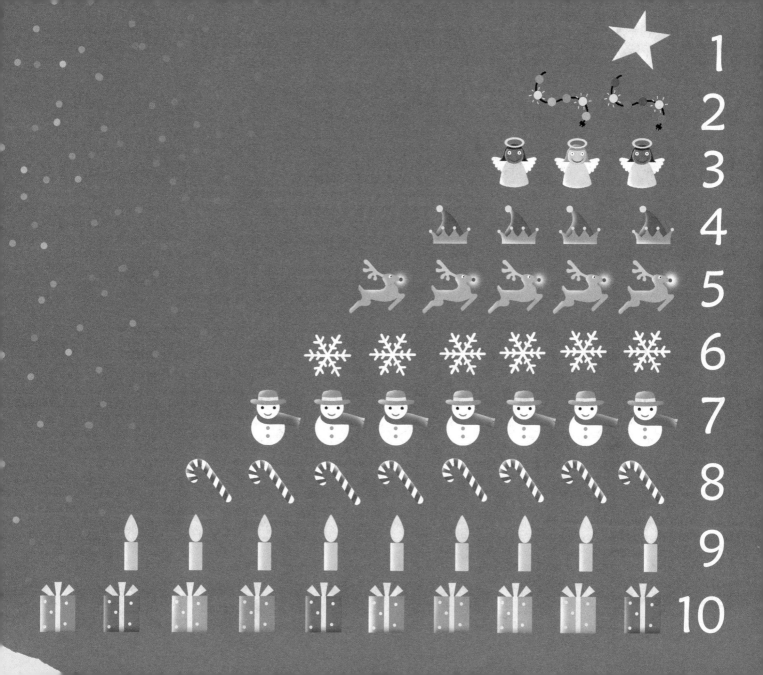

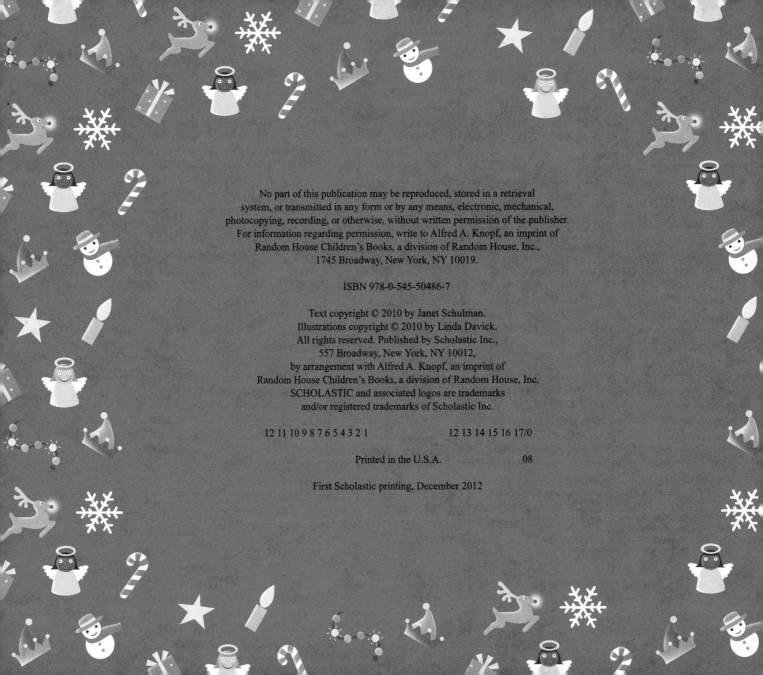

ISBN 978-0-545-50486-7

Text copyright © 2010 by Janet Schulman.
Illustrations copyright © 2010 by Linda Davick.
All rights reserved. Published by Scholastic Inc.,
557 Broadway, New York, NY 10012,
by arrangement with Alfred A. Knopf, an imprint of
Random House Children's Books, a division of Random House, Inc.
SCHOLASTIC and associated logos are trademarks
and/or registered trademarks of Scholastic Inc.

12 11 10 9 8 7 6 5 4 3 2 1   12 13 14 15 16 17/0

Printed in the U.S.A.   08

First Scholastic printing, December 2012